LITTLE QUICK FIX:

TURN YOUR LITERATURE REVIEW INTO AN ARGUMENT

#LittleQuickFix

LITTLE QUICK FIX:

TURN YOUR LITERATURE REVIEW INTO AN ARGUMENT

Robert
Thomas

Los Angeles | London | New Delhi
Singapore | Washington DC | Melbourne

Los Angeles | London | New Delhi
Singapore | Washington DC | Melbourne

SAGE Publications Ltd
1 Oliver's Yard
55 City Road
London EC1Y 1SP

SAGE Publications Inc.
2455 Teller Road
Thousand Oaks, California 91320

SAGE Publications India Pvt Ltd
B 1/I 1 Mohan Cooperative Industrial Area
Mathura Road
New Delhi 110 044

SAGE Publications Asia-Pacific Pte Ltd
3 Church Street
#10-04 Samsung Hub
Singapore 049483

Editor: Alysha Owen
Assistant editor: Lauren Jacobs
Production editor: Victora Nicholas
Marketing manager: Ben Griffin-Sherwood
Cover design: Shaun Mercier
Typeset by: C&M Digitals (P) Ltd, Chennai India
Printed in the UK

Library of Congress Control Number: 2019939530

British Library Cataloguing in Publication data

A catalogue record for this book is available from the
British Library

ISBN 978-1-5297-0125-8

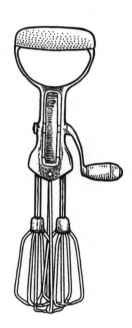

Contents

2 MIN summary

Everything in this book!

Section 1 First, you need to know what a literature review is. A well-designed and presented literature review is central to the success of your research project. Without a review we have no way of establishing where your research fits in.

Section 2 There are fundamental differences between an argument and an academic argument. General arguments can be emotional, lacking in clarity, and may never be resolved, while an academic argument should be considered, rational, logical, analytical, and above all persuasive.

Section 3 A good argument is based on what's already known. To be able to present an argument it's important to consider where the factual and theoretical underpinnings of your argument come from. Using the right data will help build a convincing argument.

Section 4 When building your argument, it's important to understand that your argument already exists within the available literature. You're not creating something original, you're just reorganizing what's out there.

Section 5 While building your argument, you must consider how to convey your argument. How you say things in building an argument will help convince the reader that your work is worthwhile.

Section 6 Your argument alone will not be enough to suggest your work has merit. The strength of your argument will need to be considered in the light of opposing views and through counter-argument. You need to provide a balanced review that will question itself.

Section 7 To make sure you're presenting your arguments properly you'll need structure. Good structure will ensure that what you present is cohesive, transparent, and above all readable.

Section 8 Making sure you're on the right track with argument development is crucial. You need a consistent plan for getting feedback and this should always be at the back of your mind.

First, you need
to know what a
literature review is

Section

1

What is the purpose of a literature review?

A

summary

The purpose of a
literature review is to
establish what previous
research has been
carried out in your
area and how that
influences your work.

summary

So, aren't reviews straightforward then?

Unfortunately not. Reviews are carefully constructed to present a comprehensive, critical, and unbiased evaluation of what is known in your chosen field. They provide a focused survey of prior research where the author identifies for the reader the main contributors, concepts, theories, and ideas that underpin their own research.

A well-executed review will identify gaps or research opportunities in a body of literature and present well-constructed, considered, and logical arguments for exploring those gaps and creating new knowledge.

CREATE A RELATIONSHIP WITH YOUR READER

Remember, you're not writing a review because you must. You're writing your review to persuade the reader that your research is worth doing. So, establish who your reader is, and then your review will indicate to them that:

- you're familiar with the literature that directly relates to your research

- you're diligent (evidence of the right reading equates to depth and that's good!)

- your work is trustworthy (using the right sources will ensure this)

- your work is balanced (this all depends on the argument you create)

- your work is worthwhile and beneficial (again, this will depend on the strength of your argument).

IDENTIFY WHAT IS GOING ON IN YOUR FIELD

You must help the reader to understand what is already known in your field. Your review will establish the boundaries of your work by providing an encapsulation of previously published works. You will need to demonstrate that you know:

- who the major authors are in the field (there may be hundreds, but concentrate on the most cited ones)

- what these authors have established and how they established it

- what the limitations are in this identified body of work.

HELP JUSTIFY YOUR RESEARCH

A review that has been carefully considered and presented can persuade the reader that your work is needed.

In doing that it should:

- provide the theoretical context of your research (essential for any reader)

- state why your research is important

- demonstrate how your research can make that all-important contribution.

PRESENT THE ALL-IMPORTANT ARGUMENT

Your review, despite setting out to support your work, needs to be written in a manner that makes sure yours isn't the only voice heard. It takes two to argue, which means two different opinions, and that's why the review is crucial: it presents all opinions relevant to the debate, and by doing this you make the case for your argument far more eloquently.

WHAT A REVIEW
SHOULDN'T BE

Great! You know what a review is. But it is of equal importance to know what a review isn't.

Be aware of the following:

- A review isn't just a summary of others' work (a mistake).

- A review isn't a description of what others have said (a bigger mistake).

- A review isn't based on what you think (a huge mistake).

- A review isn't based on one idea.

- A review isn't based on one article.

TOP TIPS

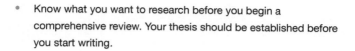

- Know what you want to research before you begin a comprehensive review. Your thesis should be established before you start writing.

- Keep you research question close. Your review needs to support it, so don't let it out of your sight when writing.

CHECKPOINT

Get it?

Q: Why is a literature review so important to your research?

Got it!

A: Because a review helps you establish, identify, sharpen, and justify your research problem, and this gives your work validity.

CONGRATULATIONS!
YOU NOW KNOW
WHAT A REVIEW IS

2 Section

There are fundamental differences between an argument and an academic argument

How can I tell the difference between an argument and an academic argument?

summary

An academic argument is an evidence-based argument that supports the research and the reason for carrying it out.

summary

Acknowledge the right writers

An academic argument accepts a broad range of opinions, ideas, and theories, from multiple points of view and perspectives, which both supports and weakens the individual's point of view.

Think of it simply: who hasn't had an argument? Everybody has, and it's normal, but too often when we argue we don't acknowledge what is being said by the other person. Usually, this is because we don't care about their opinion and we presume we're right. This sometimes can turn into an attack. Does that sound right? If it is, you're not engaging in an academic argument.

SPOT THE DIFFERENCE!
AN ARGUMENT

Here's an example of an argument

Two football fans meet to discuss whose team is better. They argue loudly, devotedly, and angrily because of their passion and loyalty to their team. They refuse to acknowledge one another's often valid reasons why their team might be the best.

Result?

We don't know whose team is better!

Problem?

Yes! We haven't addressed the main question and we don't know anything other than fans are loyal.

SPOT THE DIFFERENCE!

AN ACADEMIC ARGUMENT

Here's an example of an academic argument

Now, two academics get together to discuss whose is the better team. They begin by providing accurate facts and details; these are presented clearly, without bias, and with a view to ensuring that what they present is clear and informed beyond simple passion. The biggest difference is that academics are prepared to acknowledge one another's viewpoints to ensure they reach the right conclusion.

Result?

We know whose team is better.

Problem?

No! We've had a proper evaluation and made a decision based on fact and acceptance that there are two sides to the argument.

THE RULES
OF THE GAME

Too often when writing a review, the writer tries to convince the reader that they're right, rather than demonstrating they're right. This can become a preoccupation, particularly if the research aim isn't well established, and this method can easily descend into an aggressive approach that doesn't apply the rules of give and take.

WHAT TO AVOID

Any argument that is focused on what the individual believes they know, or thinks they know, without providing a theoretical foundation won't be successful. We call this style a polemic. You need to avoid this and here are the reasons why:

- It will read like an attack.

- It will isolate your work.

- It will isolate your ideas.

- It will convey a lack of knowledge.

- It will demonstrate bias.

- It will lack objectivity (so important).

- It will lack fairness.

- It will lack credibility.

- It will ensure you're unsuccessful.

THE ESSENTIAL SKILL

The greatest skill in writing a review is developing your argument through persuasion. You must encourage the reader through a carefully considered, focused, and, above all, true use of the literature to develop what is called a dialectic. A dialectic approach will ensure:

- you are knowledgeable

- you are unbiased

- you have read widely

- you understand your own work

- you understand your work's limitations

- you understand the views of others.

- To understand what a dialectic approach is, simply read a literature review from any peer reviewed journal.

FILL IN THE MISSING WORDS

Fill in the gaps with the correct words from the list below

persuade   convincing

multiple   polemic   credible

                        dialectic

        evidence   bias

                            emotion

The art of presenting an academic argument is to present it using
.... This approach ensures that you avoid both ....
and .... If you do this, you will avoid writing the review as a
.... This is of central importance as your work needs to be
presented from .... perspectives. In doing this, you will ensure
your review is presented as a .... And this will help the reader
to see your argument in a far more .... way. Ultimately, your
job is to .... the reader that your argument has validity and is
therefore ....

ANSWERS

The art of presenting an academic argument is to present it using *evidence*. This approach ensures that you avoid both *bias* and *emotion*. If you do this, you will avoid writing the review as a *polemic*. This is of central importance as your work needs to be presented from *multiple* perspectives. In doing this, you will ensure your review is presented as a *dialectic*. And this will help the reader to see your argument in a far more *convincing* way. Ultimately, your job is to *persuade* the reader that your argument has validity and is therefore *credible*.

A good argument
is based on what's
already known

Section

How do I begin to create my argument?

summary

You simply need to
start reading what has
already been written
and established in your
area of research.

summary

Your argument begins and ends in the available literature!

Your ability to familiarize yourself with relevant literature as soon as possible is the key to success. Reading provides the best way to develop a line of argument, but it needs to be strategic, planned, and documented to ensure you capture key themes, paradigms, evidence, and quotes that support, contradict, and oppose (yes, get used to this) your work.

LOOK TO EXISTING ARGUMENTS

A student of mine turned up stressed, anxious, frustrated, and deflated. They had spent the proceeding months trying to write something original for a literature review to ensure their argument was brand new. I asked them why they had opted for this approach and they answered, 'arguments have to be based on new thinking'.

Actually, they don't. **Arguments are based on pre-existing ideas and thoughts.** A good researcher will find those in the literature, and a diligent researcher will find gaps and inconsistencies within that literature on which to base their argument. You use other people's ideas to frame your work and take control of what they have or haven't said to support your research idea.

Originality will stem from your selection of important and relevant literature and how you present, frame, and consider those theories, ideas, and evidence in your work.

WELL-
ESTABLISHED
HISTORY

Let's consider that you want to do something totally unique. What's the issue? Well, there may not be any theory available to help you create your argument. Ensure that you are working within a well-documented, accessible, and well-defined theoretical area. It will make your research process so much easier.

Before you start, make sure you're familiar with your own research question. We covered this in Section 1, but without really knowing what you're trying to establish, the chances are you won't establish anything.

SHARPEN YOUR FOCUS

So, the trick is to know where to find reliable literature and the more reliable data that you can access, the stronger your arguments will be. You will never know everything there is to know, that's impossible and not needed for a strong argument, but you will need to know what is relevant and the more you know about what is relevant, the better!

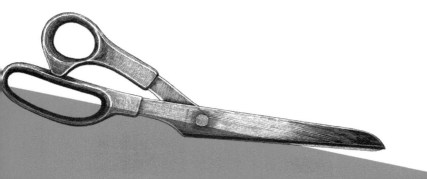

HOW DO I START?

Start your review by simply identifying potential sources of information. Consider any of the following resources to get you started. Your university will have them all in the library:

- newspapers
- textbooks
- theses

- reports
- industry documents
- conference proceedings.

UNDERSTAND WHAT YOU READ

Make sure you understand what you're reading. Make lists of key terms, words, and phrases. Build your confidence by creating your own database for each type of source you read. Using the following table will help with this.

Book title/ author	Year of publication	Key ideas presented	Key theories found	Key words established	Future reading
How to present an argument	2019	(1) Good data needed (2) Unbiased writing style (3) Need for good counter-arguments	Intertextuality	(1) Abstract (2) Intertextuality (3) Persuasive writing	Little Quick Fix series

YOUR NEW
BEST FRIEND

Good data sources should provide extensive bibliographies. Use them! A good bibliography will become your best friend as it will highlight important papers, key authors, and academic areas that you can explore in your own work. So, even with a limited amount of reading you can develop confidence, structure, and start to see your argument take shape.

Do you have a well-designed and
refined research question?   Yes / No

Are you going to be working in an
established academic field?   Yes / No

Do you know how to start building
evidence for your argument?   Yes / No

If you can answer 'yes' to all the above, then you are more than
prepared to start looking for more detailed and complex data to help
you start developing your argument.

You're not creating something original, you're just reorganizing what's out there

4

Section

How do I progress my argument?

summary

Your review will
ultimately be based on
pre-existing academic
knowledge. This
essential knowledge will
invariably be in journals
and journal articles.

summary

So, what's a journal?

If you've been diligent in building your database and in your use of
bibliographies, you'll enter the world of academic journals. You'll have
probably heard your peers and lecturers discuss using journals. They
are periodical publications that present the latest knowledge within
a given area. These journal articles will all have a review, and those
reviews will all contain arguments that you can use to inform your own.

SELECTING JOURNALS TO SUPPORT YOUR ARGUMENT

Your first foray into the world of journals might be through a generic search engine, maybe Google Scholar, and that isn't a problem, but it's so important that you avoid using poor articles and simply capitalizing on the first search.

SELECTING A QUALITY JOURNAL

Good arguments stem from being able to access good quality data. What can happen is that when people need something quickly or are under pressure, and lots of students are, they immediately turn to a search engine for quick results. This can give you superficial returns and won't help you build your argument convincingly.

So, before you decide that a journal article provides answers to your research question, consider the following questions:

1 Does the article match my research question?

2 Is it peer reviewed?

3 Has it been published in the last ten years?

4 Has it been obtained through an academic website?

5 Has it been written by an academic?

6 Has it been written for an academic audience?

7 Does it have a recognized reference list?

8 How often has it been cited? (Citations will tell you how important the work has been in developing other authors' arguments.)

9 Does it offer insight into future research opportunities?

SURVEYING THE ARTICLE

When you start to read an article, you should be considering the following and asking yourself these questions:

- What's been done? (What have they set out to do?)

- Why has it been done? (What is the rationale or argument that has driven the work?)

- How was it done? (What method was employed?)

- What was found out? (Did the research establish anything useful in the findings?)

- Where could I take it? (What are the implications for future research?)

LOOK TO THE ABSTRACT

These points might sound a little daunting at first, but you can establish all the above bullet points by reading what we call an abstract. An abstract can be found at the beginning of an academic paper.

A good abstract will sum up why the work was carried out, what was established in the work, and what its major contribution is. Abstracts can be presented differently depending on the journal, but they will all convey the same type of information.

READINGS TO SUPPORT YOUR ARGUMENT

You must make sure that an article has clearly established the bullet points on p.58. If the paper can answer the above questions, get into it! Make a record on each reading (you'll need to read an article more than once to fully understand it) of the following:

- Relevant references (anything written in the last five years will do).

- Anchor studies (what the paper cites historically to develop its own argument).

- Pertinent direct quotes that have been used to support the work (remember, somebody has already said what you want to say).

- Gaps they have identified (read the Introduction as this will always be upfront).

- Any complementary rationale that supports your work.

DEVELOP CATEGORIES

When reading journal articles, it's of critical importance that you start to categorize what you're reading, just like your initial reading. By preparing categories you're also beginning to narrow the focus of the literature you're going to use, and that's a good thing. Maybe use a table like the one below:

Authors	Rationale of the study	Theme of the study	Theories used in the study	Methods used/flaws in the study	What was established in the study	Identified gaps in the study	Most informative quotations
Jones & Jones (2015)	To explore consumer attitudes to chocolate	Gender has an impact on how chocolate is consumed	(1) Consumer behaviour (2) Gender (3) Consumer decision-making	(1) Qualitative (2) Small sample (3) Female bias (4) Nobody under 18 used	(1) Men like chocolate more than women (2) Women don't like chocolate	(1) Small sample means that this is inaccurate (2) Only dark chocolate used	'Only men like chocolate'

HOW MANY
JOURNAL
ARTICLES?

There isn't a specific number of articles that suggests you've engaged in enough reading. It isn't about how many articles, anyway, it's about the quality of the articles you read and then use to build your argument.

COULD THIS PROCESS CHANGE OR REDEFINE MY RESEARCH TOPIC?

The simple answer is yes. It's common, don't let it stress you out, and in fact it's positive and ultimately beneficial. Potentially redefining your topic means you're redefining your argument, and the narrowing down of both aspects will make your final submission stronger.

PRERSENTING YOUR ARGUMENT

Your argument will be based on existing data, so all you need is a systematic process of presenting it. This flowchart visualizes the process.

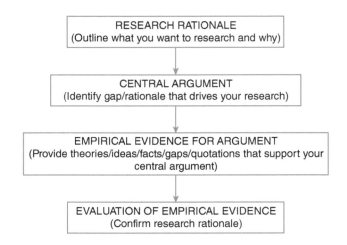

RESEARCH RATIONALE
(Outline what you want to research and why)

CENTRAL ARGUMENT
(Identify gap/rationale that drives your research)

EMPIRICAL EVIDENCE FOR ARGUMENT
(Provide theories/ideas/facts/gaps/quotations that support your central argument)

EVALUATION OF EMPIRICAL EVIDENCE
(Confirm research rationale)

TOP TIPS

- Download the Association of Business Schools (ABS list) journal quality guide if you're studying business.

- Websites such as ResearchGate, Springerlink, ESCO, Science Direct, Google Scholar, and JSTOR will cover most topics and are a good place to start for all topic areas.

- Read easier articles (use the articles' star rating to help with this).

- Don't avoid difficult or complex articles (just re-read it, and get help if needed).

- Don't rely on too few articles, but don't use too many (go for quality and not quantity).

- Summarize each contribution you read.

- Give yourself enough time.

- Keep reading (it helps with stress).

1   Search for the top ranked journals in your subject area.

2   Identify the top five cited articles about your research topic.

3   Survey the articles and assess relevance by reading their
     abstracts.

4   Broaden your search to other potentially relevant articles.

5   Develop categories to help you organize your reading.

6   Re-evaluate or refine your research topic if necessary.

CONGRATULATIONS!

YOU KNOW HOW TO PROGRESS YOUR ARGUMENT

Section

5

While building your argument, you must consider how to convey your argument

How do I convey my argument?

summary

Your argument needs
to be presented in a
measured, unbiased,
and calculated manner
that supports your
work. Anything other
than this will ensure
what you present is
unconvincing.

summary

Your writing style is the key

Your tone and writing style will have a huge bearing on the authenticity and persuasive power of your argument. Keep this in mind: 'I want to communicate, not dominate'. The communication of your argument is your responsibility, and your responsibility alone. Your words are your thoughts, and the reader will assimilate these words into their decision-making process.

GOOD TONE = GOOD ARGUMENT

Tone refers to your voice in the written work. You must remember that the reader is listening as well as reading. The reader's perception of what you're saying and how you're saying it has an impact on the success of the work.

As hard as this might be, we do need to write dispassionately, even though we're passionate about the research. When starting to present ideas, avoid emotional language and emotional words; this creates bias and we don't want that!

AVOID BIAS

Simply, bias will stop your work from being viewed as objective.
Avoid writing exactly what you think and stick to facts!

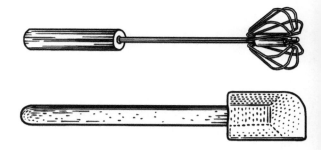

DON'T MAKE IT PERSONAL

Some researchers, to try to present a convincing argument, have been known to personally attack authors and their merit rather than critique their work. We call this Ad Hominem. If you engage in Ad Hominem it simply means you're avoiding a direct, intellectual argument and pretty much resorting to childish name-calling. Don't do it! Nobody has ever presented a compelling argument doing this.

Avoid statements such as:

- The authors are undeniably wrong.

- Prior empirical work has been flawed.

- The author is a poor academic.

- The author doesn't fully understand.

- How could the authors possibly understand?

You'll see this in poor quality articles, so be warned!

AVOID HYPERBOLE TO PRESENT THE WORLD'S 'BEST' ARGUMENT

A question that researchers ask themselves when writing a review is 'How can I present key ideas and get the reader to agree?' Well, the first thing to do is to avoid hyperbole, or intentionally exaggerating a point for effect. The best way to influence is to convey your argument through fact. Make sure you avoid using:

- personal pronouns (I, you, we)

- possessive determiners (my, your, our)

- emotional adjectives (terrible, bad, good, awful)

- emotional adverbs (strongly, clearly, completely, absolutely).

NEVER GENERALIZE (EVER)

It's often clear when a researcher hasn't read enough (and reading is the key to all of this) because they tend to generalize. When developing an argument, generalization is a distinct weakness. Avoid phrases like the ones below:

- Some authors have suggested ...

- All the research in the field ...

- Most researchers agree ...

- Most results suggest ...

- Quite a few articles consider ...

- The best academics agree that ...

DON'T GET TOO COLLOQUIAL (DO YOU KNOW WHAT I MEAN?)

Academic language isn't ordinary, it has its own technical terms and you need to be proficient in those terms to develop an argument effectively and convincingly. But you don't want to be too formal, you don't want the reader to go to sleep or need to use a thesaurus to get through your work. To counter this, some researchers write in an informal style. But this is an argument killer! Avoid this.

- Read and make notes – make a glossary of the terms other researchers use and start using that language with other researchers and in meetings with supervisors.

- Make sure you collect some good direct quotes. Somebody has always said it better than you.

Rewrite the passages below to remove hyperbole, generalization, and bias

Jones and Jones (2016) completely fail to grasp the central notion that the human self-concept is really, really important when it comes to consumer decision-making. It's incredible that they've actually missed this point because every other author says it's critical. Consequently, I believe their work should be dismissed immediately.

....

....

....

....

....

....

If you read the literature, there's a tiny body of work, by a couple of academics, that offers some insight into what the differences are between strategy and tactics. The work is so frustrating as it isn't based on anything anybody else has said, so this author won't waste anybody's time repeating it. Trust me when I say, the work I've written about is far better.

....

....

....

....

....

Some authors have questioned my main idea, but that doesn't really matter as their work was written in the 1960s. That's so long ago, and it must be obvious that that isn't relevant to a modern argument. Modern academics agree that anything written over ten years ago should be dismissed, so that's what this research will do.

....

....

....

....

....

CHECKPOINT

Get it?

Q: What is the key to an authentic, persuasive argument?

Got it!

A: Your tone and writing style!

Your argument alone will not
be enough to suggest your
work has merit

Why do I need a counter-argument?

summary

Without a counter-argument your own argument has no basis and is biased. If a counter-argument is presented well, it will strengthen your own argument.

summary

Challenge your own arguments!

The key to an argumentative (and we mean that in a good way) literature review is the need to present arguments that are against yours. This really allows you to demonstrate to the reader that you're anticipating their doubts (always a good thing), that you're a fair and balanced writer (it's essential to demonstrate this), and that you're a transparent writer (being open is the key).

You need to challenge your own work with the work of others. If you don't provide a counter-argument, an informed reader may well presume that you've strategically opted not to include relevant literature as your own work will not stand up to the scrutiny. You don't want this!

WHERE TO FIND YOUR COUNTER-ARGUMENT

The same applies to counter-argument as it does argument: counter-arguments will be contained in the literature. You don't have to create one, it will already exist. Just look in the same places:

- journals

- newspapers

- textbooks

- theses

- reports

- industry documents

- conference proceedings.

FOLLOW THE SAME PROCESS AS ARGUMENT DEVELOPMENT

Simply read and you'll soon discover that many authors will have a different opinion from yours when it comes to theory and practice and many will have provided empirical proof that will be different from what you're trying to establish.

There will be popular and highly cited papers that you can use as the basis of your own counter-arguments. Remember, counter-arguments don't have to be original. All you're doing is developing what we call intertextuality: that is, using other works to frame your own.

HOW SHOULD I PRESENT A COUNTER-ARGUMENT?

It might seem counter-intuitive but any counter-argument you present should be conveyed thoroughly, that is more than one sentence, and fairly and objectively. You should approach creating a counter-argument in exactly the same way you created your central argument: with depth and transparency.

WHAT SHOULD BE IN IT?

A counter-argument should present factual and potential flaws in your argument and could be based on:

- alternative theories that do not support your position

- a lack of agreement on your major ideas

- concerns with method

- established thinking

- academic tradition.

DON'T GO OVERBOARD

Do not commit to a 50/50 between your argument and counter-argument. Balance is key in presentation (tone) but not volume. A paragraph, even several sentences, is appropriate when presenting a potential counter-argument.

What is essential is that you demonstrate to the reader that you've considered all aspects of your research question and you need to establish positive and negative evaluations of it.

HOW DO I PRESENT IT?

This is where lots of researchers can go wrong. It's very important that you convey to the reader that you're about to go in a slightly different direction. The following phrases can help start a paragraph that contains a counter-argument:

- However, a review of the literature indicates that …

- Despite the above, the work of Jones and Jones (2013) and Davis (2015) offers a contrary opinion to the central ideas of this research …

- Authors, including Smith, Smith and Evans (2013) and Green (2016) have suggested that there is a lack of evidence for …

- Williams and Jones (2016) have encouraged debate that reflects flaws in the current understanding relating to the main theories in this work …

- In the following section the academic uncertainty surrounding the central debate will be considered …

COULD THIS CHANGE MY ARGUMENT?

It might, but don't worry. If you read or find something that you think damages your argument, it will most probably turn out to be positive. Here's what to do:

- Speak to your supervisor for advice.

- Refine/modify your research question.

- Refine/modify your literature review.

What you'll probably find is that an incident like this, and the reflection that will come from it, will strengthen your research. What's the lesson? Don't worry about discovering something that you subjectively think is a problem; it probably isn't!

DO I RESPOND TO THE COUNTER-ARGUMENT?

Yes! We call this a rebuttal. A rebuttal is simply the writer finding doubt in the counter-argument and in turn strengthening their own argument. It's all about give and take. Like your counter-argument, your rebuttal should be introduced appropriately. The following phrases can help introduce your rebuttal:

- While the work of Jones and Jones (2013) offers insight, their contribution fails to explore ...

- The work of Green (2016), while important, has failed to find universal support in the extant literature, and it does not clarify its position methodologically. This leads to the following evaluation ...

- It is important to acknowledge the work carried out by Davis et al. (2015), the rationale for their study was based more on assumption that fact ...

- But a review of the authors work leaves several relevant questions unexplored ...

YOUR REBUTTAL

Just like your argument and counter-argument, your rebuttal should be:

1   based on fact

2   non-emotional

3   respectful

4   supportive of your argument

5   concise.

MULTIPLE CHOICE

Cricle the correct answer

What is the purpose of a counter-argument?

A   To flesh out your review

B   To present additional arguments
     that may not correspond with your own

C   To impress your supervisor

D   To show you can read complex ideas

What should a counter-argument should be based on?

A   Different opinions

B   Conjecture

C   Fact

D   Intuition

Where should you look for your counter-argument?

A   Online

B   Upstairs

C   The library

D   In the existing literature

CHECKPOINT

 What should a counter-argument convey?

A   You are a brilliant researcher

B   You are an objective researcher

C   You are a subjective researcher

D   You are a careful researcher

 What is the best way to present a counter-argument?

A   Quickly

B   Briefly

C   Evidentially

D   Sparingly

 What is the purpose of a rebuttal?

A   To refute opposition to your argument

B   To use up your word count

C   To enhance the quality of your writing

D   To create a standalone argument

A
C
B
D
C
B

ANSWERS

7

To make sure you're presenting your arguments properly you'll need structure

How can I make sure I'm creating strong arguments?

summary

Present a logical flow to
your review, highlighting
all claims and counter-
claims throughout.

summary

Engage your reader using good structure

The secret to a solid, structured review and argument is to know how to pace your argument and when to introduce the counter-argument. Academic writers often forget they're simply telling a story, and like any good story its purpose is to keep the reader engaged, interested, and unable to put the book down.

Your reader will be interested in what you've written about, will expect to see expertise and a command of the subject area, and will want a few twists and turns along the way. So, like all good books, we need structure because good storytelling is based on that.

WHAT SHOULD THE BASIC STRUCTURE BE?

Structure presents a significant issue when introducing other opinions, as the main drives for completing a review can be based on establishing what you want to do and why. That is important and should never be overlooked.

FOLLOW THE FORMAT BELOW AS A BASIC PATTERN:

1   **Research rationale** – express what you're doing and why.

2   **Central argument** – offer the general thesis of your argument.

3   **Present evidence** – present your main argument here, and the reasons why your argument might be successful.

4   **Counter-argument** – acknowledge your opposition.

5   **Rebuttal** – challenge the counter-arguments.

6   **Conclusion** – sum up your main argument and move on to the method.

WILL STRUCTURE CHANGE?

This format will be present in every peer reviewed journal article you read. The more you read the more familiar you'll become with it. When you're writing it's important to have a conceptual map, so use the one below to help you visualize what you need to do. As you'll see, it's like the one in Section 4, so you're already familiar with the idea of a linear story.

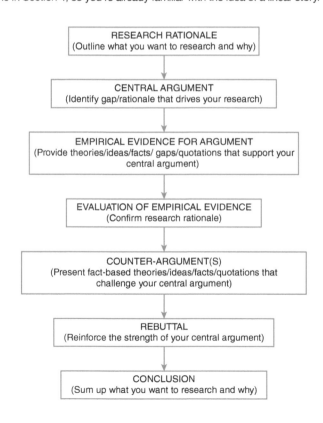

RESEARCH RATIONALE
(Outline what you want to research and why)

CENTRAL ARGUMENT
(Identify gap/rationale that drives your research)

EMPIRICAL EVIDENCE FOR ARGUMENT
(Provide theories/ideas/facts/ gaps/quotations that support your central argument)

EVALUATION OF EMPIRICAL EVIDENCE
(Confirm research rationale)

COUNTER-ARGUMENT(S)
(Present fact-based theories/ideas/facts/quotations that challenge your central argument)

REBUTTAL
(Reinforce the strength of your central argument)

CONCLUSION
(Sum up what you want to research and why)

DOES THE COUNTER-ARGUMENT COME AT THE END?

It doesn't have to, it can come anywhere, but think about the story.
Make sure you present your argument fully before you present your
counter-argument.

*Thinking about your own
research project, answer the
following questions*

Research rationale: What makes your research worth doing?

....

....

....

....

....

**Central argument: What is the central argument that underpins
your work?**

....

....

....

....

....

**Provide empirical evidence: Where does the main evidence that
supports your argument come from?**

....

....

....

....

....

**Forming the counter-argument: Who are the main authors and what
are the main theories that make up your counter-argument?**

....

....

....

....

....

HOW TO CREATE YOUR STRUCTURE

Rebutting the counter-argument: What is the central idea that underpins your rebuttal?

....

....

....

....

....

Conclusion: What lasting impression would you want to leave with your reader?

....

....

....

....

....

Q : What are the six elements of structure?

....

....

....

....

....

....

Answers

Research rationale, central argument, evidence,
counter-argument, rebuttal, and conclusion.

Making sure you're on the right track with argument development is crucial

Section

8

How can I win my argument?

summary

Remember, the point of
an academic argument
is not to win in the
traditional sense, but
to own the debate and
convince the reader that
your work has value.

Your aim should be to make a valuable contribution to an ongoing debate

The secret to winning this academic argument is the realization that the argument you're presenting is, in all probability, an ongoing argument. Too many researchers make the mistake of committing to their argument very early in the research process, writing the review, and then patting themselves on the back when it's done. This is quite natural, but don't do it. During the months between drafting your review and submission, ask yourself, 'What's going on in my area?'.

WILL SOMETHING NEW CROP UP?

In short, yes! If you remember, journals are periodical, that is they are published regularly, and this potentially means a regular influx of new data that may offer support to your argument. This is positive and realizing that there might be new knowledge out there that can help you should be enough motivation to keep on searching right up until submission date.

The temptation is to sit back and pat yourself on the back because you've produced a solid review, robust argument, and your supervisor has told you it's good. However, the reality is that while you're enjoying a bit of down time, arguments are being reshaped, reconsidered, and there are new contributions to your field.

PLAN FOR CHANGE

It's a mistake to think that the debate stops because you've stopped writing. New articles will be produced and you will need to know that they're out there. **You must have a timetable in place to capture new academic contributions** to help with argument and counter-argument.

TOP TIPS

1 Check your key words every two weeks (these should already be
   established).

2 Check general databases every two weeks to see if there are new,
   contemporary developments.

3 Check for new empirical contributions every month in your
   specialist journals.

4 Continue the process of documenting your new reading.

5 Keep revisiting your review, as time away from it will help you see
   it more clearly when you return.

YOUR FIRST DRAFT WON'T BE YOUR LAST DRAFT

Given that you're going to keep on reading, this will pretty much ensure that you keep on writing. Your review won't be finished until you submit. Multiple drafts will be needed before reaching the final version and this is normal practice. However, never delete a draft. Even if you're frustrated and want to start over, do not delete your work. Every sentence will have value and it's only feedback that can establish this.

GET FEEDBACK

A mistake lots of researchers make is that they don't get regular feedback. We can often write in a bubble and presume what we're doing is correct. It may well be, but feedback at regular intervals is a key to success. Consider that:

- you will never have the final evaluation of your own work

- you won't grade your own work

- your supervisor will be a fount of knowledge (it's true, they are)

- this may be your first review, it won't be your supervisors!

YOUR COMPLETION CHECKLIST

To help establish if you've completed your review and developed an argument, work through this simple checklist:

1   You've gone full circle with the literature, and you're reading the same articles you read at the beginning.

2   You've read everything you can in the allotted time frame allowed (even though there's always something new).

3   You can summarize your argument and counter-argument in a few sentences.

4   Your supervisor is happy!

This is a journey every academic, researcher, or thesis student has been on. It isn't a unique journey, but this is your journey and there are four C's to keep in mind on this journey:

1   Conceive (what is my research?).

2   Construct (have I supported research with evidence?).

3   Convince (have I persuaded the reader with my evidence?).

4   Counter (have I opposed my argument?).

CONGRATULATIONS!

YOU ARE READY TO START WRITING

To make sure you can produce the best argument possible, work through the following questions

☐ Do you know the main purpose of a literature review? If not, go back to p. 9.

☐ Can you clarify the differences between an argument and an academic argument? If not, go back to p. 25.

☐ Do you know what a good academic argument should be based on? If not, go back to p. 39

☐ Have you understood the best sources to use when constructing an academic argument? If not, go back to p. 53.

HOW TO KNOW
YOU
ARE
DONE

CHECKPOINT

☐ Do you know what writing style leads to an effective, persuasive academic argument? If not, go back to p. 73.

☐ Do you know why counter-arguments are so important to defining your own argument? If not, go back to p. 91.

☐ Do you know how to structure your argument to make it as strong as possible? If not, go back to p. 109.

☐ Do you know why it is so important to keep reading right up until the point of submission? If not, go back to p. 123.

Glossary

Abstract A brief summary of a research article.

Academic argument An evidence-based discussion of your research position.

Ad Hominem A personal, written attack on an individual author.

Bias A personal belief that shapes your opinion of something.

Contradiction A process of reasserting your point without acknowledging the merit in another argument.

Contribution New information provided by a journal article that is seen as adding to current knowledge.

Counter-argument An argument that is created to oppose an idea or theory that has been created in another argument.